THE AUCTIONEER'S

APPRENTICE

A PARABLE FOR LIVING AN
ABUNDANT LIFE

CHAD COE

The Auctioneer's Apprentice

A Parable for Living an Abundant Life

Chad Coe

Gavel Publishing
2018

First Printing: 2018
ISBN 978-0-359-23788-3

Dedicated to my awesome wife, life partner, and wisdom teacher, Jill.

-1-

Wake-up Call

The cell phone was ringing, rattling Sam Paige out of a sound sleep. Scrambling in the dark to find the device, he knocked over a bottle of water, soaking the magazines that lay in a heap next to his bed.

"*Dammit,*" he whispered, his fingers finally locating his phone and seeing that it wasn't his alarm that was going off, but an incoming call from his boss.

"Uh…hello?" Sam answered, full well knowing who was on the other end.

"Sam, where in the heck are you? Do you have any idea what time it is?" insisted Lonnie who was his shift manager at the supermarket.

Feigning ignorance as he swung his feet out of bed and smack dab onto the wet floor he answered, "No, Lonnie I don't know what time it is. I set my alarm, but it must have been for 5 p.m. instead of 5 a.m.," he stammered.

"Jeez, Sam, this is the third time this month that I've had to call you. It's 6:30 in the morning; you should have been here half an hour ago. I mean you only live like less than a mile away, and I don't understand…"

Sam cut him off before the rant added to his waking headache.

"Lonnie, *Lonnie* stop; I will be there by 7 and work later than my shift if you need me to, okay?"

Lonnie let out a long groan, emphasizing his disgust at having to talk to a 40-year-old man like a teenager and finally said, "Fine, just get in here!"

Sam put the phone down and surveyed his small bedroom as his eyes had finally adjusted to the darkness. It was early spring and while it was getting lighter earlier, the shades had been drawn tight as usual. Getting up to head to the bathroom, he had to maneuver around a half-eaten, foot-long sandwich he had grabbed at the deli before he left work the night before. The sub was loaded with processed meats that gave him serious indigestion, so he tossed it aside and somehow overnight it had slipped off the nightstand on to the floor. The room reeked with the smell of cheese and cold cuts.

He had a short thought about gnawing on the remaining half of the sandwich for breakfast, but a slight gurgle in his gut changed his mind.

As the shower got hot, Sam stared into the mirror as he did every morning with nearly vacant eyes reflecting nothing but an inner anguish that had long ago replaced any sense of hope that his life would be any better than it was right now. He had grown accustomed to his life where one day simply melted into the next. With little money in the bank, even while working upwards of seventy hours a week, Sam stayed at the supermarket longer than needed just so he didn't have to spend so much time alone by himself and the unending stream of negative thoughts that cascaded through his brain like a toxic leak.

Sam Paige was a short, stocky man with a growing spare tire around his midsection, a mess of dark hair that he rarely combed, and a scruffy beard that he wore just because he didn't think shaving mattered much anymore. Most of his time away from work was spent reading crime novels or endlessly flipping channels until he grew tired enough to fall asleep. Over the years life had taken a toll on him, the erosion of a broken childhood, a failed marriage, and more than a few wrong turns had bent him beyond what he thought was possible. He had become a man who was devoid of any sense of self or hope, just another cog in the wheel of life waiting to die.

He shivered a moment as the mirror began to fog up from the hot water steaming down in the shower. He thought he saw something flash in his eyes, a sliver of light that seemed to come and go in an instant. Rubbing the glass clear, he looked for the illumination again, but there was nothing but two bloodshot orbs with deep brown pupils and large bags staring back at him. Sam grunted slightly, got into the scalding shower, and tried once again to wash off the rust of his existence.

As he quickly dressed for work, he listened to the small transistor radio's traffic reports and coverage of politics and crime, but just before launching into sports the announcer declared, *"Today is Saturday, April 21, 2018, which among other things is designated as National Auctioneers Day, a tribute to those fast talking, quick minded folks who not only entertain, but inspire action. The National Auctioneers Association estimates that nearly a quarter-trillion dollars in goods and services are sold by professional auctioneers each year. While the concept of auctioneering is about 2,000 years old, the chatter like cadence is uniquely American, and it is thought to have become popular starting during the Civil War..."*

Sam was busy pulling himself together, so he barely heard the proclamation as the words bounced off the tile walls towards his ears. Quickly shutting off the radio before the announcer could finish, he took one last look in the mirror and headed out the door.

There was no way Sam Paige could possibly have known that in less than 48 hours his life would change drastically and beyond all odds, he was going to get a chance to begin again.

-2-

Opportunity in Disguise

Lonnie was waiting for Sam at the timeclock.

"So, even on a Saturday you can't make it on time, huh? Just punch in and get to work," Lonnie hissed in a snake like fashion, as he drummed his fingers on the metal wall slot that held a slew of timecards.

Sam just looked at the floor manager, who reminded him of Barney Fife from *The Andy Griffith Show*. As he put his yellow name card in the machine, he thought to himself, *"I'd rather punch you out!"* while smiling at his boss. Lonnie departed and Sam made his way towards the produce department to start unpacking the morning delivery. As he cut through the deli section, a warm and cheerful voice called out to him.

"Well, good morning, Sam."

He stopped in his tracks and turned to see the smiling face of Jill Rand peeking from behind the long refrigerated display case filled with cold cuts, cheeses, and prepared meals.

Her voice always made Sam stop what he was doing.

Jill smiled and took advantage of the fact that no customers were waiting with ticket in hand this early in the morning, so she excused herself from behind the counter. She wiped her hands on the store issued apron and then pushed back a stray blond hair from her face. She had piercing blue eyes and a quick smile, in spite of the fact that there had been much sorrow in her life since her husband died five years earlier. A single mom, she worked long hours for minimum wage, mostly for the insurance. While she was slight of stature, Jill Rand was strong in all the right places and for the right reasons. She had quit her high paying corporate PR gig when her husband was diagnosed with cancer so that she could be with him. As his illness worsened, so did their finances and by the time she had to say goodbye to Paul there was little left to work with. She sold their big house for far less than it was worth, moved with her college age son Jarrett to a small apartment, and after being unable to find work back in the corporate world took a job slicing meat at the supermarket that was just a mile from home. After being alone for the better part of five years, Jill had put much of her grief behind her, so when she met Sam, she felt like there just might be more to him than meets the eye.

"Sam how are you?" she asked.

"I'm late Jill. That's how I am," Sam responded, wishing he could take back the words that sounded a bit harsh.

"Oh...I see," Jill said. After a moment she decided to head back behind the counter, but there was something on her mind that she needed to take care of and now was as good a time as ever.

"Uh...Sam, are you busy on Monday evening?" Jill asked.

"What do you mean busy?" Sam answered, shifting from one foot to another, starting to feel uncomfortable.

"Do you have plans on Monday evening is all?"

"Well, I might have to work late you know, because basically that's all I do."

"Well, here's the thing. I am going to a benefit dinner on Monday night and wondered if you might like to be my guest?" Jill offered, feeling a bit relieved that she finally said something to Sam besides, "Krakus ham is on sale again."

"I might have to work Jill. But what is this benefit for?"

"It's a fundraising event for cancer research and I get invited every year since Paul died. Matter of fact, the only time I've ever attended was with him," she said, her voice trailing off. "Thought it might be time to go back, but really don't want to go alone, and I wondered if you might go with me?"

As he stood there in the deli section surrounded by bacon, cheese, and piles of packaged meats, Sam knew that he had better make up his mind quickly. He liked Jill, maybe even more than he might admit, but the thought of showing up at an event because her husband died made him uneasy. Besides he thought to himself, Monday night is pizza night, and I might have to work and...

Before he could answer, Jill stepped in.

"Sam, I didn't mean to put you on the spot. I'm sorry. It's really not a big deal. Maybe next year." Jill said, her voice now almost a whisper.

And with that, she gave him a smile, wished him a good day and went back behind the counter just as Mr. Barrow, one of the regulars, showed up for his pound of German baloney and Longhorn cheese.

Sam took a deep breath, a bit relieved that he didn't have to decide and wandered off to the produce section where there were three crates of oranges, tomatoes and lettuce waiting for him.

It wasn't long before Lonnie was over his shoulder.

"Paige…"

"Yea?"

"Paige what's your problem?"

"Like I said, my alarm didn't go off and…"

"No, you bonehead, that's not what I am talking about."

"What then?" asked Sam.

"I was in the bread aisle and heard Jill Rand ask you to be her guest for an event on Monday night. What are you stupid? I mean c'mon man. Jill from the deli asks you out? What's wrong with you? She's a widow, good looking, and basically you have no life outside of avocados," Lonnie snapped, hands on his hips.

"There's nothing wrong with me Lonnie," Sam pushed back as he busted open a box of navel oranges. "I am usually pretty busy on Monday nights and I might have to cover a shift or something."

"You don't have to work Monday night. What you will do, like you always do, is leave here, go home, order a pizza, watch mindless television, wallow in your '*my life sucks*' wading pool, and fall asleep on the couch. Then the next morning I will be on the phone waking you up and you'll be late for work just like today!"

Sam pretended not to hear.

Lonnie grabbed his shoulder, surprising Sam and making him take a step back.

"Sam. You don't want to miss this opportunity with Jill. It might not come around again. Not sure why I am telling you this and frankly I couldn't care less if you go, but I am telling you...*don't blow it*. Clean up your act, get out of your cave and go to the event. If you don't take Jill up on her offer, someone else will, I can guarantee it," Lonnie said. "Think about that while you stack lettuce, oranges, and tomatoes. But, don't think too long; Jill is only working until noon today."

Lonnie, satisfied with his lecture, spun on his heels and went back to the bread aisle to chew out the new kid about the proper procedure for rotating stock.

Sam went about his work quietly as he always did, robotic in his movements that had been practiced a thousand times before. Time passed quickly and soon enough it was time for a break. He tossed the last few heads of iceberg lettuce into the bin, grabbed the empty boxes, and made for the backroom to toss them. As he threw the boxes in the dumpster he decided to take an extra few minutes downstairs in the employee break room. As he descended the stairs, he could hear the sound of someone weeping.

He turned the corner into the room and there at the table sat Jill...*crying*. The room was stark white with glaring overhead lights and a metal table and chairs that screeched on the floor when they moved.

She hadn't seen Sam as her eyes were covered, so he cleared his throat.

"Oh great," Jill spat. "Just great. First, I ask you out and get turned down and now you catch me balling my eyes out. I am much better at cutting meat then I am at asking you or anyone else for that matter, to simply be my guest on Monday. It's not like I want to jump in the sack or..." Jill stopped herself in mid-sentence. "I'm sorry Sam. This isn't about you."

Scratching his head and messing up his hair even more than usual, Sam squared his shoulders and said, "So, what is the event for again?"

Jill dabbed at her runny nose with a napkin and said, "It's a fundraising dinner. You know a buffet kind of thing that people pay for and then they do a raffle, I guess, and an auction. I think they are even having an auctioneer at this one. You know someone who actually uses a gavel and stuff."

"Auctioneer? Where did I just hear that?" Sam thought to himself.

"So…uh…well I talked with Lonnie and he told me that someone else would work overtime if needed on Monday night. So, if you would still like to go, I mean I don't have a car but I can meet you there you know. I can pay for my ticket and you can pay for yours, and that way we can pay, you know, for the tickets." Sam stammered.

Jill's bright blue eyes cleared, she wiped her nose again and pushed back the stray blond strand of hair that wandered across her brow. Taking a deep breath, she finally said, "Sam, that would be wonderful. I can meet you there, no problem. Are you working tomorrow? I can leave you the direction."

"Yea, I'm working tomorrow." Sam said.

The room suddenly became quiet. Jill stood up and nodded to Sam and grabbing a blue spring jacket off the hook made her way up the stairs.

Sam stood in stunned silence.

"What have I gotten myself into?" he thought to himself. "I wonder why she was crying?" was his second thought.

With just a few minutes left on this break, he put a dollar into the soda machine, pulled out a can, and sat down on the hard metal chair to ponder all that had happened since he overslept.

-3-

Silent Auction

After he got off work, Sam spent the rest of Sunday getting his act together. It had been quite some time since he put any effort into his appearance. He hit the Quick Cuts Shop and spent $15 on a haircut. On the way back to his apartment he stopped at the local Goodwill and was able to find a nearly new suit that fit for $25. He topped it off with an Arrow brand white collared dress shirt that was just $2.99 that someone with a size 16 neck had donated. The shirt had one small stain on the inner sleeve, but Sam figured no one would see it, so for less than $50, he would look presentable at the event.

Inside, however, he was a wreck.

A million questions were flooding his mind, none of which had any real answers. It had been years since he was on a date and was this an actual date anyway? Do I sit on her right side or left side? Does it matter? What if she asks me to dance? Is there dancing at this thing? Do I have to donate money? I mean I already spent almost $45 just to look good. Am I supposed to bid on some auction item? Have I ever been to an auction? How many other people are going to be at the table? What if they start asking me questions about where I work? What am I going to tell them?

Sam Paige was at a crossroads, something he had so often tried to avoid. By accepting Jill's invitation, he put himself in a situation that demanded decisions and actions, both of which in the past had never turned out well for him. But he had to go, no matter how much turmoil he felt in his gut.

Before he knew it, Monday had rolled around. Apparently, Jill was off but he got a lot of looks from everyone else at the store. Word must have spread about the impending "date" and he tried his best to just mind his own business. Even Lonnie, who was usually obnoxious, actually gave him a thumbs-up sign just before Sam punched out for the day.

The haircut looked good, a close shave revealed a face he hadn't see in a long time, and while there were more than a few worry lines, his eyes seemed a bit clearer again. Soon enough, the sound of a taxi horn beckoned, and off he went to what he was sure would be a very long night.

He rarely left his neighborhood and so after greeting the cabbie and giving him the address of the banquet hall that was about a thirty-minute ride, he settled back and took in the sights.

Sam had nearly forgotten there was a world beyond his small boxed-in life. Perhaps it was the haircut and new duds or the fact that his pattern of pizza night had been interrupted, but he had a few small pangs of "aliveness" as he watched people hustle and bustle along, so many of them talking on an iPhone or listening to music with earbuds, two things Sam had almost no experience with. A rudimentary flip-phone for an emergency and that battered AM radio in the bathroom was the extent of his technical participation.

The cabbie was silent during the ride except for a few curse words under his breath when he got cut off in traffic, but the GPS in the car had been correct and just shy of thirty minutes they rolled into the parking lot of Windemere Restaurant and Banquets.

"There sure are a lot of cars here," Sam mumbled under his breath. People were streaming into the main entrance in droves, the men all looked handsome and the women were dressed *"to the nines"* as his mom used to say, alluding to their well-coiffed hair and beautiful outfits.

All of a sudden, a moment of panic set in. *"My God,"* Sam said out loud, *"I don't belong here."*

With that the cabbie swung around and said, "Wait, what sir? This is the correct address you gave me."

Sam met the cabbie's eyes and said, "No, this is the correct address and I am supposed to meet a friend here for an event but…" His voice just trailed off.

After spending time with hundreds of fares the cab driver quickly understood Sam's hesitation.

"Sir, may I offer you a word of advice?"

Sam just stared back at the man.

The cabbie said, "My favorite author is Emerson. I did a research project about him in college many years ago and two of his quotes has stayed with me all these years. May I share it with you?"

Sam just nodded his head up and down in silent agreement.

The cab driver raised one hand and with great authority said, *"Always do what you are afraid to do. Do not go where the path may lead, go instead where there is no path and leave a trail."*

Satisfied with his delivery, the cab driver let the words hang in air for a moment and followed with, "Now then, do you want me to take you back home?"

Sensing the moment, Sam took a deep breath and said, "No. I'll go in."

"How much do I owe you for the ride" he asked, digging in his worn wallet for cash.

"Nothing. This one is on me. This is my cab, I am my own boss and today you gave me the chance to recall a very important time in my life. I was able to quote the great Ralph Waldo Emerson!" The man seemed very pleased with himself.

The cabbie smiled and stuck out his hand. Sam managed a lopsided grin and shook his hand.

As he stepped out of the cab, he heard his name being called.

Sam turned around and there was Jill.

Time seemed to stand still. The moment was surreal.

There she was walking towards him looking incredibly beautiful, her blonde hair framing a wide grin on her face;

and now outside of the supermarket's antiseptic background and glaringly bright overhead lights, she was simply *illuminating.*

"Well, hello there handsome," Jill said. "You clean up pretty good."

Sam shifted on his feet back and forth, not used to getting a compliment.

"You look really good, Jill. Almost didn't recognize you without that hair net and smock," Sam offered, trying to sound sincere.

Smiling, she hooked her arm in his and together they followed the flow of guests inside the building. Finding their name tags on the check-in table they made their way to their seats.

It was soon apparent that neither Jill nor Sam knew anyone else in the room.

But that was about to change.

As their table filled up and everyone made introductions, the chatter grew in the room and a rising tide of infectious good energy pulled Sam in a direction he hadn't felt for a very long time. There were ten paddles on the table, each one with a number and the guest's name on the back of it. Jill explained that those would be used for bidding during the live auction portion of the evening. He picked his up, turned it over and there was a large **#14** printed on the paddle.

Sam felt his shoulders and hands relax. His right leg that was usually moving up and down with nervous tension was quiet. Glancing around the banquet hall he saw nothing but smiles, hugs, handshakes, and light flooding in from the big windows.

The tables that were set up at the far end of the room were filled with all sorts of things; patrons were moving from each item to the next, putting numbers on pieces of paper. Finally, his curiosity got the better of him and he asked Jill what they were doing.

"Those are silent auction sheets," she said. "People are bidding on the donated items and you use your number to bid, Sam. It allows people to bid and then outbid each other for whatever they are interested in. At the end of the night the number that has the highest bid is the winner."

"I see," Sam responded, nodding his head.

"Do you want to take a look at some of the items?" Jill asked.

"Sure."

Sam and Jill got in line and began to weave their way around the room, stopping here and there to look at what people were bidding on and for how much.

The items ranged from auto detailing to abstract art to autographed sports memorabilia, and one item in particular caught Sam's eye.

"Wow, Jill, look at that! A baseball signed by Ernie Banks!" he said loudly. "Mr. Cub!" Sam reached out to the cube that held the baseball. His fingers gently tapped on the plastic.

Jill had never seen Sam so animated and excited.

"Are you a baseball fan?"

"Well, sorta. When I was a kid, Ernie Banks was an idol to me. You know, he seemed like a really good guy and of course, a great baseball player. I was never any good at baseball, but I sure liked to watch him play. He just seemed so happy all of the time."

Sam was transforming right before her eyes, getting younger and more in touch with his deep inner self all because of an autographed baseball.

"Why don't you put a bid on it Sam?" Jill asked. "The sheet says the minimum bid to start is just fifty dollars."

The thought of bidding which was about the same amount he paid for his haircut and clothes, at once seemed ludicrous, but sensing that he needed to make a move, and confident that someone would outbid him, had him nodding in agreement.

Feeling confident he wrote, **"#14- $50"** on the sheet.

"Wow," said Sam. "That's the number Ernie Banks wore on his uniform."

Jill simply smiled.

"You don't have to chase success. Take care of yourself in mind, body and spirit, and affirm your intentions; then success will find you."

-4-

The Promise

Soon the dinner was in full swing.

It was obvious to Sam that most of the people in the room had, in one way or another, been touched by cancer. Many were like Jill who had lost someone they loved, others had lost friends and people they knew from work. The conversation at their table confirmed his thoughts as pictures of those who had passed away and those still battling the disease were passed around.

There were more than a few tears.

But even in the midst of sadness, there seemed also to be a bit of hope as they knew by attending the event and raising money for research that perhaps someone else might be spared the pain that was the common denominator of the evening.

When the food was served, Sam glanced at Jill who instantly understood what he was communicating.

"Outside fork first, for the salad and then the next fork is for the main course," she whispered with no hint of sarcasm. Sam nodded a silent thank you.

While the room was alive with the sound of conversation, clanking plates, and laughter, Sam would glance to see if anyone else had bid on that Ernie Banks baseball. There was a steady stream of people back and forth to the auction tables so it was hard to tell if another bid had been made. Too nervous to go up and look, Sam tried to engage in the table conversation as best he could, but it was difficult as he was Jill's guest, and this was her place to connect, not his.

And, connect she did.

Even though she didn't personally know anyone at the table except Sam, Jill felt a kinship with those who were sharing dinner and stories about the experiences that they had and the losses they'd endured. It had been a very long time since she felt she could "open up" about losing her husband at such a young age, and this was a safe space, even though she knew that when the event ended, she might not see these people again until next year.

Sam watched Jill carefully, pushing aside his own concerns about attending, and he was able to read between the lines a bit of how important it was for Jill to be in the room that night. As he so often did, he tended to only see things from his side of the fence and judge others, not fully knowing their story. Jill had been in severe pain for quite some time and this event was the perfect antidote. He sat back, ate slowly, and listened to Jill talk about her life, gaining more respect for her with every word she spoke.

Soon after the main course had been consumed and the tables were cleared by the waitstaff, the carts of great looking cakes and other delights appeared. But before the goodies were fully wheeled out a man stepped up to the podium, tapped the microphone to test it, and then stood silent until the room became still.

The auctioneer had taken his place on the platform.

The man was six feet tall, nattily dressed, but not "over the top." His dark hair was slicked back a bit and his bright eyes darted about the room, making contact with the five hundred people in attendance. While he had all the trappings of a successful man, his face also bore the lines of change, indicators that he had paid his dues many times over, which gave him an air of authenticity that could not be bought or sold.

The first thought in Sam's mind was that the man looked like a combination of a 1940's film star and pitchman from a late-night commercial for some miracle cleaner.

Either way, he was a commanding presence.

Suddenly and without warning, the man slammed his gavel down. A booming *craaack* rang out as the sound of hardwood maple striking the podium filled the room. Both Sam and Jill, along with a few others in the crowd, jumped a bit at the sharp noise.

The man at the podium took off his expensive suit coat and handed it to a pretty girl who was standing just off to the side. With all eyes upon him, he slowly rolled up his sleeves, cleared his throat once, and began to speak.

"Ladies and gentlemen. My name is Max Farber, I am your auctioneer for this evening, and I thank you on behalf of the Cancer Alliance for your willingness to participate and support this worthy effort to raise a significant amount of money that will go directly to research and development to fight cancer."

The crowd burst into applause, startling Sam nearly as much as the gavel did. "When I said significant money, I meant *significant…money…*" said Max with a broad smile, drawing out the words for effect.

For the next hour, Max Farber worked the room like a surgeon, extracting incredible amounts of cash as hands holding paddles shot up in a feeding frenzy of bidding. Auction items ranged from a vacation in the Bahamas, to a private dinner with a Hollywood celebrity, to a guitar autographed by a rock star, to VIP seating for two at Wrigley Field that included a limo ride and time in the dugout before a Cubs game with the players.

After each auction item was sold Max would slam down his gavel and yell to the room, *"WINNER!"* to which the crowd would echo back, in unison, *"WINNER!"* to his announcement and applause would break out. The auctioneer was not just working the room, he was working up a sweat and his energy was infectious. Sam noticed that people weren't so much outbidding each other, they were actually participating in a one-of- a- kind event where they all felt like winners.

When Sam realized the "Cubs Experience" included a skybox for ten people at Wrigley Field, with a full buffet and autographed items for each fan was sold for $5,000 or 100 times the amount he bid on that Ernie Banks baseball, he could hardly believe his ears.

"Who has that kind of money?" he thought to himself.

Turning to look at the winning bidder, it was a man just about Sam's age with a broad smile and a twinkle in his eyes, probably brought on by the fact that he wasn't just going to see the 2016 World Champion Chicago Cubs, but that he was able to contribute to an important cause at the same time.

Sam joined the crowd in applause for the man, caught up a bit in the energy of the moment. He turned and looked at Jill who once again had tears in her eyes. Instinctively he reached out, placed his hand on hers and gave it a squeeze. Jill wiped her eyes, gave him a wink and smiled.

At the podium, Max stood off to the side for a moment. A spokesperson for the Cancer Alliance stepped to the microphone and thanked everyone for attending the gala event and said that the silent auction items would be closing in just ten minutes and then there would be one last live auction item before the evening ended.

People stood up to stretch their legs and check on the silent auction items they had put bids on. Sam found his way to the baseball and realized there was only one more bidder for it in the amount of $60.

Another pivot point for Sam.

He quickly calculated in his head what his finances looked like, how much his next paycheck would be, and since he had already spent money on clothes how could he afford to rachet up the bid? What if he bid $65 and someone outbid him? *"Better to be disappointed now rather than later. It's kind of the way life goes for me,"* he thought. The energy of the previous hour left him and his shoulders slumped a bit as he walked back to his seat. Jill noticed his demeanor; she asked about the ball, but Sam didn't respond.

It was her turn to give his hand a squeeze.

The moment was interrupted by the smack of the gavel once again.

"So, we come to the final auction item of the evening ladies and gentlemen. It is one of those times we can actually say, we saved the best for last," barked Max. He was walking slowly back and forth on the platform, his eyes even brighter than before in anticipation of what was to come.

"I have here in my pocket an envelope with a piece of paper in it. It is in some way a 'mystery' prize in that I am not going to tell you what is on that paper until the bidding has ended. Remember what we are gathered here for tonight, what the mission is, and that the commitment is to raising research money in the name and memory of those whose lives have been cut short and altered by the insidious disease of cancer."

The room was silent as a stone.

"All I will tell you about what is on this paper in my pocket is that it represents the most valuable gift we have to offer each other and ourselves, it is perhaps the most coveted commodity in the world."

A few audible '*ahs*' rose from the crowd as the intrigue grew.

"So, who will bid $1,000?" Max began.

Three bidding paddles shot up in the air.

"I have one thousand dollars here, who will make it three thousand?"

Six paddles this time.

"Number 188 was first up. Who will make it five thousand?"

Now four paddles rose high above the heads of the bidders. "Number 22 thank you; we have five thousand, who will go to ten thousand dollars?"

A gasp and a few laughs were heard as Max doubled the amount in an instant.

"Ten thousand dollars? I know you're out there, who will give me ten thousand?"

No takers.

Max went to work, "Are you telling me that there isn't one among you who isn't ready to make a ten-thousand-dollar donation? I know there is someone in this room who is ready to do this. I can feel it. I will tell you what I know in my heart of hearts. Ten thousand dollars will not only change the life of someone stricken with cancer, but...*your own life as well."*

Sam couldn't believe what he was seeing and hearing. The frenzy of the room was back to full tilt and people were bidding on something they couldn't even see!

Standing with his hands on his hips, sweat on his brow, and a determined look on his face, Max stood at the podium and said once again, "I have five thousand in the room...*WHO WILL GIVE ME TEN THOUSAND DOLLARS*?!?!?!"

The room fell silent...Sam's jaw dropped open.

Jill's paddle was in the air.

"I have ten thousand in the room! Number 13 right up front here! Ten thousand dollars!" Max cried.

The room exploded, but Sam hardly noticed.

Max thought about pushing a little more but something inside him said that this was far enough.

"Ten thousand once...ten thousand twice..........
SOLD FOR TEN THOUSAND DOLLARS!"

The man had just sold Jill piece of paper tucked in his pocket for what would take Sam six months to earn at the store.

His mind reeled and the room became a blur.

Max then revealed the contents of the envelope, holding up a small blank piece of paper over his head. The crowd once again grew silent.

"This blank paper represents the possibilities that each of us literally have at our fingertips. Life is a blank slate that we get to fill in every single moment of every single day. Let us not forget the reason we are here tonight and those who are not. Let us remember that there is no guarantee that we'll be here tomorrow, so let us fill the blank space before us the very best way we can."

And with those words hanging in the air, Max brought the evening to a close with a sharp slap of the gavel on the podium.

-5-

The Gift

The room was still buzzing after the final gavel had dropped on the auction.

Sam was collecting his thoughts that had been scattered about; he felt like a whirlwind had swept through the banquet hall. The energy was electric and palpable, and when he finally gathered himself, he looked at Jill. As he began to speak, she cut him off.

"Sam. Sam. I did it! I made good on the promise!" she chirped loudly, clapping her hands together. "I DID IT!"

Realizing that Sam had no idea what she was talking about, Jill put her hand on his shoulder and looked him square in the eyes.

"Sam. My late husband Paul and I were at this fundraiser for cancer research just six months before he passed away. We were so taken with the people here and what they were doing that he made me promise…" and as Sam had witnessed twice before, Jill began to cry. But suddenly she caught her breath, wiped the tears from her face and continued, "Paul made me promise that I would use

$10,000 of his life insurance policy as a donation to the cause of cancer research at this very event. But in the years since he passed, I couldn't bring myself to attend until that day I asked you to join me. I needed someone to come with me so I could follow through. I didn't know how I was going to use the money, but when the auctioneer talked about that blank piece of paper, I knew I had to be the winner!"

Sam just sat quietly

"My life has been an empty space since he passed away. I don't really like the job at the deli but it keeps me busy, and when I first met you I decided then and there at some point I would ask you to be my escort. This was finally the year I kept my promise to Paul. I couldn't have done this without you."

The room was an ebb and flow of activity, but Sam noticed none of it. He could barely believe what he was hearing.

"I cannot thank you enough, Sam. I turned a major corner tonight." Jill smiled. As if lifted up by unseen arms, Jill rose from her chair and pulled Sam up with her.

"Let's go claim my winning piece of paper!" Jill shouted.

Quickly, Jill led Sam by the arm through the throng of people and they soon found themselves in a line at the platform because Max Farber was holding court at the podium, surrounded by the event organizers thanking him for helping raise a record amount of money.

With beads of sweat still running down his face, Max was slowly rolling down his sleeves when he caught sight of Jill. Excusing himself from the group, he strode up to Jill and said, "Well, the ten-thousand-dollar lady! I am guessing you are here for your blank piece of paper! Well done and bravo!"

Jill smiled broadly and said, "Mr. Farber, my name is Jill Rand, and I will gladly give you a check for $10,000 in exchange for that paper you have in your pocket on one condition."

Max tilted his head a bit and said, "Well, Jill Rand, first-off call me Max, and secondly, what condition might that be?"

Jill said in a calm, clear voice, "The one condition is that you write down the most important lesson you have ever learned in life on that piece of paper. I am going to have it put in a little frame and it will be a constant reminder of this incredible evening."

Max grinned, took the paper out from his pocket, and walked back to the podium. Picking up a pen, he looked back at Jill, wrote something on the paper, carefully folded it up, and walked back to where they were standing. He handed the folded paper to Jill who accepted the note and clasped it in her hands tightly, almost prayer-like.

Sam stood off to the side in silence, watching the scene unfold when suddenly Max's voice put him at attention.

"I'm Max Farber."

It took a moment or two for Sam to realize that Farber was talking to him, with his arm extended.

"I'm Sam," came the reply followed by a hesitant handshake.

"Good to meet you Sam. Did you enjoy the evening?" Max inquired.

"Not really sure what to say Mr. Farber. This is the first event of this kind I have ever attended. Very exciting but not sure what to make of all this. I mean raising money for a good cause is important, but people buying things for so much more than they are worth and…"

Before Sam could continue, Max Farber cut him off.

"Sam may I ask you a couple of questions?"

Jill eyed both men, wondering what was going on.

"Sure, I guess," said Sam.

"What do you do for a living, Sam?"

"I work with Jill," Sam said, hoping he wouldn't have to admit he worked in the produce section of a supermarket.

"Great, but what exactly is it that you do to earn a living?" Max persisted.

"I work in a supermarket," Sam said in a tone just above a whisper. "In the produce section."

"Great, now then, how much do you get paid per hour to work in the produce section at the supermarket?" Max continued.

"I make fourteen dollars an hour. I've been there a long time," Sam shared, trying to sound professional about the whole thing.

"So, that's great Sam. Congrats on your longevity. But you don't make fourteen dollars, you earn it. There is a difference. After taxes, it's what more like ten bucks an hour? Do you think you are worth more than that Sam? I mean would you like to earn more money?"

"Well, of course I would," Sam shot back. "Who wouldn't?"

"Great! So, who decides what something or someone is worth, Sam?"

The question Farber posed went into Sam's mind like an arrow.

"What do you mean who decides?"

"Well, who decided that you should earn fourteen dollars an hour? Did you decide that?"

"Of course not. My pay is set by the company."

"But you would like to earn more, yes?"

"Yes," said Sam.

"But, how will you ever earn more money if you allow someone else to decide what you are worth?"

By now Sam was starting to sweat. He was feeling a bit of anxiety with Farber's line of questioning, and he was sure the whole room was listening in. Jill was just a few steps away, arms folded, clutching that piece of paper.

"Sam, when I am on the platform auctioning off items to raise money for a cause, I am insisting that the value of what I am having people bid on is priceless, because in many ways it is. These people are here to raise money. They know they are going to spend money and with the understanding that each of us ultimately decides the value of everything."

Sam just stared at Max.

"Sam did you bid on anything tonight?"

Seeing him in a bit of a situation, Jill answered for him, "Sam did bid on an item tonight. He is a big Chicago Cubs fan and Ernie Banks was his favorite player. Matter of fact the number he had for auction bidding was #14, the same jersey number Mr. Banks wore!"

Sam nodded a silent affirmation.

"Did you win the ball, Sam?"

A quick look to his left at the table where the ball had been placed showed an empty spot. His shoulders slumped and his back bent a bit forward. That old feeling of losing crept up his brow.

"Apparently not."

Farber slowly began to wipe his forehead with a colorful handkerchief and asked, "Sam how much did you bid on that ball?"

"Well, since it was my first auction and I don't have a lot of money because I don't earn a lot of money, I just decided that I would do the $50 bid which was the minimum."

"I see," said Max. "Why didn't you bid higher?"

"I don't have a lot of money because I…" Once again, the auctioneer cut him off.

"Yes, Sam I know. However, do you know what the retail cost of a baseball is? About fifteen bucks on a shelf if you want to buy one. That means balls probably cost Major League Baseball about three or four bucks each wholesale. That baseball, however, was signed by one of your heroes, the great Ernie Banks. A ball signed by 'Mr. Cub' can be sold for two hundred dollars or more! You could have had it for far less but were afraid to bid even though he means a great deal to you. Someone determined the value of that ball more than you did. Do you know what the ball signed by Ernie Banks went for in the silent auction tonight?"

"No…no, I don't," replied Sam.

"Sixty dollars. Ten dollars more than your bid or the same amount you earn after taxes for an hour of your time."

Sam was again very quiet, absorbing what was being said to him.

"Do you know how I know that?" Farber pushed.

"Because you are the auctioneer?" Sam replied.

"No…*because I bought it.*" Max said.

Now Jill's mouth was hanging open and she steadied herself on Sam's shoulder.

"Ernie Banks was one of my heroes too. His name on that ball has great meaning to me, the memories of him at Wrigley Field playing first base are priceless to me as well," Max said wistfully. "Of course, I had no idea that you had bid on it as well until you told me."

Sam wasn't sure if he should laugh or cry. All he knew is that he was feeling very odd about accepting the invite to this dinner, he would never see Jill the same way again, and he was silently kicking himself for not keeping an eye on the ball, in a manner of speaking.

As a steady stream of people began to file past the front of the room and towards the exits, Max reached under the podium. He slowly pulled out a bright white baseball encased in a small cube. There it was, autographed in bright Sharpie marker, *"Ernie Banks #14 Chicago Cubs."* The auctioneer held the ball up to bright ceiling lights, which infused it even more with illumination, brought it close to his chest for a moment, and with a wide grin splitting across his face he stuck out his hand and pushed the ball right next to Sam's heart.

"Here you go Sam. Enjoy."

Sam Paige nearly fainted.

"You are giving me the ball you just bought?"

"Yes, I am."

The only response that Sam could muster was "*Why?*"

The auctioneer took a step back, shuffled a few papers on the podium, reached for his jacket, and in one measured move, put it on. He pulled up his shirt collar a bit and straightened his tie.

"Because I have decided that ball is worth more to you than it is to me, Sam."

Jill started quietly crying; the whole evening had been far more than she could ever have expected.

Sam took the small plexiglass cube in his hands, and a feeling of gratitude swept over him like a waterfall. He simply smiled; it had been a very long time since he had something to smile about. His *inner boy* leapt with joy, and he clutched the ball like it was made of gold.

Max pulled a business card out of his pocket, gave it to Sam and said, "I am having lunch at noon tomorrow at my favorite restaurant. If you can get away for an hour, I will send a car to pick you up. Lunch is on me and I will have you back before the tomatoes realize you are missing," Max laughed. "Deal?"

"Why…uh…but why would you buy me lunch? You just gave me a baseball."

"Because there is something I want to share with you, and it might be of great value. Of course, you will be the one to decide how much value."

Not one to ever deviate from a schedule, he was mulling it in his mind when he felt a sharp jab in his ribs.

It was Jill.

She leaned over and whispered in his ear. "Sam, I have a feeling this is a one-time invite and you need to go tomorrow."

Suddenly the words of the cabbie were also in his ear.

"Always do what you are afraid to do. Do not go where the path may lead, go instead where there is no path and leave a trail."

Sam set his jaw, put one hand out to Max and said, "I would be honored to join you for lunch tomorrow." He might get chewed out for a long lunch but getting gnawed on from Lonnie was nothing new.

"That's great Sam. Just text me the address of the supermarket, and I will take care of the rest. I look forward to seeing you as well." Max spun on his heels and was gone in an instant.

With that, the spell was broken. Sam was fully aware that the room was nearly empty, and that Jill was standing really close to him.

As they walked towards the front door, Sam couldn't help but again admire the baseball a few times, and when Jill stopped to thank him for coming with her, it was Sam's turn to ask a question.

"Jill, what did Max write on that paper you paid ten thousand dollars for?"

She realized in all the excitement she hadn't yet looked. Jill slowly unfolded the paper and with an unsteady voice read out loud, "*What lies behind us and what lies before us are tiny matters compared to what lies within us.*"

This time it was Sam's eyes that filled with tears.

They decided that they should share a ride back to the city as both of them were mentally, physically, emotionally, and spiritually exhausted. They rode back in silence. The only sound was the light evening rain on the windshield of the cab.

One question kept repeating itself in Sam's mind all the way home.

"Who decides what something is worth?"

"Most people base their value on what they <u>own</u> rather than who they <u>are</u>. If you don't know who you really are, you will never appreciate how valuable your presence is in the world."

-6-

Curveball

Sam texted the address of the store to Max before he went to sleep, fully intending to slip out at lunch and discreetly meet the cab in the parking lot without anyone catching sight of him. However, when he woke up the next morning, his fears started to creep back in.

What if someone saw him leave? What if Lonnie was in the parking lot for some reason? What if traffic was bad and he was really late? What if he got fired for going to this lunch meeting? And, on top of that, he didn't even know where he was going.

What if?

Just then his cell phone rang…it was Jill.

"Uh, hello Jill," Sam muttered. "How are you doing this morning?"

"I am more than great Sam," Jill chirped. "Have you recovered from the big night? Did you sleep with that baseball? Are you ready to meet Max at lunch?"

"Recovery might take some time. I am still not exactly sure what happened, but I'm glad to have been there when you made that bid. That was really something. I didn't sleep *with* the baseball, Jill," Sam said while looking at the cube that he placed on the nightstand next to his bed. "As far as lunch, I am having second thoughts."

"Really?" Jill asked.

"Yes, really. I don't know this guy at all, and while he was pretty incredible to watch at the event, I don't want to get involved with something that seems to be maybe more than…and I don't know where the lunch is…what if Lonnie sees me get in the cab and then what if I …"

"SAM! STOP IT!" Jill demanded. Once she realized that she had his attention she quietly said, "When was the last time you took a sick day?"

"Uh…uh…I think it was last October. Yeah, last year."

"Call Lonnie and take the day off, Sam. Go to that lunch meeting."

Sam thought for a moment and replied, "You think I should?"

Jill took a deep breath and said, "No Sam, *I know* you should."

Five minutes later Sam gave Lonnie a call, begged off for the day, and while Lonnie put up a little resistance just to push back, he figured that the night out with Jill must have been too much for Sam, so he finally relented.

Sam immediately texted Max the address to his apartment and explained the change. The response from Max was to the point.

"Great! Car will pick you up. Regards, M."

Sam was still considering cancelling just a short time later when a large, black sedan pulled up out on the street and put its flashers on. Looking out the window his text tone rang.

"Car for Mr. Sam Paige parked out front, sir, thank you."

Sam did a double take, grabbed a light jacket and locked the door behind him. The driver got out of the sedan, opened the back door and said heartily, "Good day to you, Mr. Paige. My name is Seth, I will be driving you today."

Sam was in serious overwhelm. First, all that went on last night, and now a private car for a guy who worked stacking cucumbers and shuffling boxes of avocados?

The ride was a quick 20 minutes, and when the car pulled up outside of The Red Ram, a high-end restaurant that

Sam had once read about in the food section of the Sunday paper, he took a deep breath and quietly exclaimed, "Whoa."

"Yeah, Mr. Paige this place is incredible. All the big hitters in town come here for lunch and dinner."

Sam simply nodded and thanked Seth, and just before exiting the car he said, "Uh, pardon me, do you know how I am getting back home?"

"Yes, sir. I will be waiting for you when you are finished having lunch with Mr. Farber," Seth answered.

Sam nodded again and closed the car door behind him. He walked from the bright sunlit day into the foyer of The Red Ram, and there was Max to greet him.

"Well, Sam, how was your ride?" Max asked, extending his hand.

"I was expecting a cab, not a limo," Sam smiled as he shook Max's hand.

"Ah…low expectations can often lead to more than expected, if you get my meaning" said Max.

"Not really, no," said Sam.

Max just smiled and said, "Let's eat."

The main dining room of The Red Ram was filled with people who were noisily talking, dressed mostly in business suits, a sharp contrast to Sam, who didn't want to wear the same new clothes two days in a row, and was wearing jeans, but was glad he put on a collared shirt. Max was dressed in what had to be a tailor-made suit, but without a tie. They closely followed the maître d' through the maze of tables and now and then someone would reach out to Max or call his name and he would respond with a smile, a handshake, or a thumbs-up.

Sam started to understand the magnitude and presence of this man who had invited him to lunch, and the looming question of *"Why Me?"* came forth again.

Finally, they made their way to a smaller room in the back corner of the restaurant. There was a small alcove with a table in it, maybe four feet long with a chair at both ends. The walls were lined with bottles of wine behind glass doors and the room was lit from one very expensive looking hanging light fixture that seemed to make the deep dark wood of the table appear to be floating in air.

"Only one way in and one way out of this room," Max chuckled.

Sam managed a weak smile as the maître d' pulled out his chair while Max made his way to the opposite end of the little space. After being seated and a bottle of sparkling water opened, Max quickly said, "Pick anything on the menu. Everything here is top-notch, Sam. I am so very glad you were able make time available for me today."

As Sam was looking over the menu, he said, "Max, can I ask you a question?"

Max looked at Sam and said, "You want to know why I asked you to lunch today, right?"

Sam nodded a silent yes.

"Well, Sam, the truth is that I know you, because you remind me of someone I once knew."

"What does that mean?"

"There was a time when I was not who I am today, but rather I was how you are now. I mean that with no offense because you are just operating on what you believe to be true about life. When I met you at the event last night, I had a flashback of sorts to a time in my life when things were very different."

Sam just stared at Max. "Go on."

"Again, I mean no offense, but I am very aware when I am around someone who has become a product of his circumstances. I used to be that way too."

Sam leaned in a bit and took a sip of the bubbly water in his glass.

Max took a deep breath and said, "Up until third grade I was in 'special ed' class with three students, no desks, and a teacher with a cattle prod to keep us in line. My first time for any sort of traditional reading or math came in fourth grade and the problem was that I never '*learned how to learn*.' I was never any good at math, so when someone finally gave me a calculator, my world changed. Sam do you know what I do for a living?"

Sam was now rigid in his chair, eyes wide open and mouth dry. "Auctioneer?"

Max leaned back and said, "No, Sam, auctioneer is my *calling*. My *career* is in wealth management."

The room suddenly got even smaller as Sam couldn't believe what he was hearing.

"For a while I really believed that I belonged in that special education class. While my learning curve was much longer than most kids, eventually I was able to *'train my brain'* and even though from first to third grade I was not up to speed, in the long run I figured out a way to overcome that. Patience became a priority for me, and it has taught me that long term success is possible. So many people miss opportunities because they are impatient."

Max beckoned the waiter who took their orders. Sam chose a grilled hangar steak with mashed potatoes and salad, while Max ordered salmon with baby red spuds and broccoli.

By now Sam had given up on any last reservations he had about meeting *"the auctioneer"* for lunch. As their food was being served Max said, "After we eat, I will answer all those questions swirling around in your head."

Sam grabbed a fork, and before he took his first bite, he had an overwhelming feeling that he needed to pay attention as never before.

-7-

Pivot Point

It was a delicious lunch with small talk to fill time but when the conversation turned to the baseball signed by the great Ernie Banks that Max had given Sam as a gift, there was a palpable shift.

"Max, I am still stunned that you just gave me that baseball. I don't remember a time when I have been given a gift that meant so much to someone else, but was still passed on to me. It really was very thoughtful."

"Sam," Max barked, "as I said last night, each of us gets to determine the value or meaning of just about everything. One person can lose a job and to him it means the end of his life; and for someone else who loses a job, it's the beginning of a new life. As for that baseball, I know it's where it needs to be, and that is a great gift to me as well, so we both win."

Sam nodded in the affirmative. "Max, part of me hates to admit it, but you were correct that you see yourself in me, at least up to a point. I never endured special education classes, but I was a poor student in school and spent most of my summers at a desk to make up for failing classes during the year, which just made things worse I think. While my friends were out having fun in the summer, I was in school, and I grew to hate learning. My parents divorced when I was nine and I was tossed back and forth between these two very angry people, so I learned to just be quiet and go along with the program. I never really learned how to express myself or my feelings about almost everything. I never went to college, but I did spend three years in the Army which taught me some important lessons, none of which I could see while I was serving. I married when I was just twenty, but within four years we were divorced. I found work here and there, trying to make ends meet, but sometimes it seems they never do. I found this job at the supermarket close to my apartment and eventually I gave up, mostly on myself, I guess."

Max was listening intently.

"So, in many ways I just accepted that there was little I could do about my life, and even though I was miserable inside, I pretended '*things were just fine.*'"

"Ah, the '*lie of fine*' that is one of the worse things you can believe," Max said.

Sam shook his head. "*The lie of fine?*"

Max said, "Yep, the number one lie we tell ourselves is that we're happy when, in fact, we're miserable. We self-destruct and our confidence level is low. We're frustrated. We have no outlook for where we're going or how we're going to get there. And, we feel like we're on this journey, on a solitary path. Feeling alone in a world of seven billion people is a disease of the mind, a horrible, debilitating disease that the ego feeds off of and one that pushes you into a downward spiral."

"How do I start to reverse that spiral?" Sam asked, surprised that the words came so easily.

"Do you make your bed in the morning when you get up?" Max asked. The question made Sam blink twice.

"Uh...no...I...don't," Sam responded.

Max continued, "Do you have a morning ritual that includes some sort of meditation, contemplation and goal setting for the day to come?"

"My morning ritual is waking up usually after hitting the snooze button a couple of times, jumping in the shower with the news on, and then walking to work. That is, of course, unless I oversleep like I did Saturday, and my boss has to call to wake me up!" Sam recalled.

"You want to change your life? Then start with making your bed."

"Are you kidding me? That's the way I begin to reverse the downward spiral of my life?"

"Sam, it's not about the bed, it's about accomplishing something, every day that starts to retrain your brain before you even begin the rest of the day. Add to that a few minutes of meditation which can be a simple as sitting for a few minutes...*with the radio off*...and just being thankful to be alive. Gratitude goes a long way in creating what I call, *The Abundant Life Roadmap*, for living life on purpose. It has four different parts: first and foremost, it's about finding out what your personal values are, what's important to you. I use a staircase approach, taking it step by step. It's basically about finding your altruistic best self and that's done by asking yourself better questions and discovering what's important to you and then building on that. So, if what's important to you is to be able to have financial success, I would ask you, what's important *about* having financial success? Is it: *I want to be able to be content, as I define it*; I want to be able to give back to the universe; and, I want to be able to leave a legacy for my family, my children, my friends."

"I don't believe I have ever thought about those things much, if at all," Sam responded, still trying to imagine his bed made every morning.

"Most people don't, Sam," Max said. "They don't set goals, they don't blueprint their lives in any meaningful way. Something magical happens when you take your thoughts and put them on paper or on a white board so you can see them. It helps you keep your focus on what you deem important. I have a huge white board in my office with my *Life Roadmap* on it. There are detours, and often I have to wait in traffic and sometimes in construction zones, but the map is critical to living an abundant life."

"Abundant life…now there is a concept that seems out of reach to me. I mean, I work, go home, work, go home and that's about it." Sam said wistfully. "I cannot imagine my life any other way than it is right now."

"Therein lies the solution to your current situation!" Max exclaimed. "Let me ask you a few questions Sam."

"Sure."

"Could you ever have imagined that Jill would ask you to an event? That at the event you would be witness to people donating money in sums that would take you months to earn? That the very person who invited you would pay $10,000 for a blank piece of paper, and that I would give you a baseball signed by one of your heroes?"

"No way," Sam replied.

"And yet, even though you really never considered any of that happening, all of it did take place. It happened. Do you know why?"

"No."

"Because you showed up. You got outside of your narrow comfort zone and said '*yes*' to something new. You agreed to participate without knowing the outcome and that kind of '*faith,*' for lack of a better term, put things in motion that were dormant."

Sam was now leaning on the table, oblivious to the sounds of the restaurant patrons behind him. "Go on."

"One of the first things to do is ask this question, '*What does your ideal life look like five years from now?* ' So, you must take the time to look at your life personally and ask where are the roadblocks on your life map? Where are the frustrations and how do you remove them so that you can live your dream?"

"Live my dream? I don't even know if I've ever had a dream for my life."

"Sam, you are in the perfect place, know it or not, believe it or not, to create a life that is far better than the one you are living now. A blank slate if you will, that has started to fill itself in because you went to a charity auction. Look at all that has transpired in just a very few hours."

Max continued.

"I know that you have strengths that are forgotten and weaknesses that you constantly remind yourself of. Most people operate that way. There is an old saying, *'What you focus on the longest becomes the strongest thing in your life.'* So much of our conversation is about focus and perspective. The results you experience are directly in line with what you believe to be true about yourself and your place in the world. If unpacking boxes of tomatoes brings you joy, then do it. If not, then why are you at the supermarket? Because it's a job? Back to imagining your life in five years. Does it look the same as today? If it does and that thought makes you depressed, then you are heading in the wrong direction. The only person who can do anything about that...*is you.*"

Sam had never heard anyone talk like Max Farber spoke.

"Max, Jill shared with me what you wrote on that piece of paper she paid for. So, is it today when I begin to figure out what truly lies within me?"

Max sat back in his chair, looked at Sam and said, "Two things. First, in my opinion Jill didn't 'pay' for that piece of paper, she made good on a promise, so that's important to remember. And, regarding your question...*that is up to you.*"

For the first time that he could remember, Sam felt like his life had some possibility, some sort of meaning, vague as it might be.

Max then said, "Are you ready for the main course?"

Sam looked at his plate that was devoid of food and seemed confused.

"What I mean is, are you up for some concepts and ideas that if consumed, will set you on a new life path?"

"Yes, I am," Sam grinned.

"True abundance is about living three lives. It's your personal life, it's your professional life and it's your financial life. When you can put all three in balance and are able to live them on a daily basis, the end result is happiness."

-8-

The Choice

Just as Max was about to begin, the waiter showed up with a cart of sweet treats for dessert.

Max said, "Sam, make your choice," in a voice that carried with it a sort of subliminal message.

Suddenly, Sam felt like what he ordered for dessert was more important than ever before. He hesitated because he rarely if ever ate out, and for sure, dessert wasn't something he spent money on.

Max sensed his hesitation.

"Don't order much in the way of dessert, do you Sam?"

"Nope. I kinda just stick to the basics."

The waiter remained patient, swaying slightly as he observed the two men.

"Sam, what was your favorite dessert as a kid?"

Sam thought about it for a second, and recalled a time when he was on a school field trip that ended up in an ice cream shop. The place was filled with all sorts of goodies to be had, but Sam didn't have any extra money to buy the one thing he really wanted…*a banana split*…so, he settled for one scoop of vanilla in a cup.

"Well, I've always wanted to have a banana split ever since I can remember," Sam replied, sparing Max the details.

"You've never had a banana split?" Max asked, his voice full of amazement.

Even the waiter raised his eyebrows.

Sam shrunk a bit in his chair.

Before Max could issue the order, the waiter cleared his throat and said, "Sir, we don't have banana splits on the cart, but I would be happy to have one made in the kitchen for you…*if you wish*."

Max grinned, Sam nodded his head yes and the waiter bolted to the kitchen.

"Sam, I know that there is a lot coming at you in a very short time, but a simple thing like dessert and making a choice about something you might enjoy, but usually don't allow yourself to, speaks volumes to your self-worth, my friend."

With that, Max took out a small book from his inner coat pocket and pushed it across the table.

Sam picked it up and looked at the title.

"The Power of Peopletizing. Networking Your Way to An Abundant Life." by Maxwell Farber.

With a confused look on his face, Sam started to speak, but Max cut him off.

"PEOPLETIZING!" Max barked with a practiced voice. *"Linking people through thoughtfulness, caring, sharing, and mentoring; a genuine, strategic, compassionate way of connecting people that works to everyone's advantage; building relationships in order to purposefully help one another; acknowledging and learning about people informally in order to avoid the 'dance' of cold selling."*

"Made up the word myself," Max proclaimed.

Sam looked at the word again, then back at his host.

This time, before he could speak, the waiter showed up with the most impressive banana split Sam had ever seen. It looked like something in a magazine ad. It was an incredible creation with three huge globs of vanilla, strawberry, and chocolate ice cream, with the banana slices sticking out from both ends of the boat-shaped pewter serving dish. Chocolate sauce was running down in rivulets, and it was topped off with a mountain of whipped cream and a Maraschino cherry perfectly placed on each peak.

Sam's eyes widened with a full-face smile.

The waiter placed the superb concoction in front of Sam who grabbed the large spoon, and in one quick movement, took a huge chunk out of the masterpiece and shoved it in his mouth, forgetting that he wasn't a ten-year-old, but a fully-grown man at a very fancy restaurant.

Looking up with chocolate on his chin, both Max and the waiter were grinning as well. They all broke out in laughter.

"You go ahead, Sam, dig in. I'll talk, you listen. My dessert today is watching you enjoy yourself."

Sam was good with the deal.

Max continued.

"Peopletizing has helped me create a life I cherish, a life in which I am able to make a difference in the lives of others. It's a life philosophy that developed as I built my business and founded a children's charity. It's about investing in relationships in all areas of life. It's about getting to know people. It's about developing mutually-helpful connections that allow everyone involved to capitalize on the talents, skills, and abilities that create great businesses, generous not-for-profit organizations, and loving families.

I've learned over the years that helping others always comes back to me. Life isn't about 'stuff,' it's about 'people,' and it seemed to be the perfect name for it."

Sam nodded and continued savoring his dessert.

"The adults who helped me through a childhood defined by learning disabilities were sowing the seeds of my philosophy long before I articulated its concepts. I started from a place where I always had to try harder and work harder—and not give up—and so I know that it's beliefs, not events, that shape our lives. Countless people contributed to who I have become. Even now I continue to discover that every day is an opportunity to help others—and that *who you are* is more important than *what you have*," Max said with deep conviction.

Max then went into greater depth about his journey. "Attention Deficit Disorder would have been my label when I was a kid. But at that time there was no formal or specific diagnosis. There wasn't anything 'special' about my education, it was basically for kids with difficult needs. No homework. No tests. Really, just custodial care. My days were filled with playtime. I was disorderly, sometimes even wild, you could say, and I never felt like I was learning anything. I was very outgoing and desperately wanted friends, yet felt like I didn't fit in. In addition to the fact that I didn't go to school with the kids in my neighborhood, my family frequently moved and peer connections were few and far between. Just before I was scheduled to start fourth grade I broke my leg and was in the hospital for six weeks. When I returned to school, I was on crutches, not exactly the initiation to mainstream education that I was hoping for, and school was difficult. I was enrolled in remedial programs and every day I received one-on-one help. In the school library dedicated adults worked with me on reading, math, and writing. They were in so many ways, 'angels' in a sense, because without them, I might have remained as I was, and lived under that 'special ed' label my entire life," Max recalled.

"When I was about seven years old, my mother became a 'secret' alcoholic. That brought along with it a lot of violence and tumult in our family. Eventually my parents divorced and my brother, sister, and I went to live with our father. While I was often the class clown and frequently involved in playground fights, it was during those transition years that I began to develop a greater sense of self and to function independently. I took care of myself; I got where I needed to be by hitchhiking or riding my bicycle. I realized that I was going to have to work hard and take nothing for granted. Perhaps my greatest discovery was realizing that when I was challenged, I did better in school!"

For about the hundredth time since meeting Max, Sam couldn't believe what he was hearing. His pre-conceived notions about the man were rapidly changing with every word.

Max knew he had Sam's full attention, in spite of the banana split that was now downed by half.

"High school provided more than academic lessons. I also played on the tennis team. The lessons of tennis are still with me today: focus and strategy are paramount to succeeding, winning, and getting what you want. Tennis also gave me friendships-and a sense of belonging. When I was 16, I started working, took college entrance exams and, best of all, met Katie. I started a window washing business and worked as a caddy when there were no window washing jobs. The CEO of Bally's Gaming was the first person I caddied for; he took me under his wing and taught me the fine points of caddying. To this day, I still can't believe how nice he was to me. It's something that I haven't forgotten and try to *'pay it forward'* whenever I can. When I met Katie, I liked her immediately. We became great friends and dated throughout high school. Rather than noticing my deficits, Katie offered me support and understanding. She saw my potential, when most everyone, including me at times, only saw my flaws. Even though my ACT and SAT scores weren't great, I eventually earned a Bachelor's Degree in Business at the University of Illinois. I was, and still am, very proud of that."

Sam had never been very comfortable around "college educated types" but Max was sharing so much of his own journey that once again, Sam had to think about how often he judged people without knowing their story.

"During college and after, I engaged in a variety of small business ventures that taught me a great deal. Each was interesting and exciting and provided opportunities for learning. Though I had no sales experience, my first business was traveling from city to city selling jewelry at flea markets. That endeavor was the first of several attempts in the retail business, all of which provided important business lessons, but not much income. Katie and I eventually married and had three children. There were difficult times, for sure, and rising above them was always a challenge. Not always easy to do, but essential in my growth as a person. However, the greatest training ground for my current career came through State Accounting, a family business founded by my grandparents. During the ten years that I worked at State Accounting, I modernized and computerized processes, expanded the client base through marketing, managed more than two hundred business relationships, and personally completed more than four hundred tax returns every year. I learned much in that period of time, the most important of which was dealing with people from all walks of life. The experience gave me a perspective that kept me from judging others by the money they earned or spent," Max concluded.

By now Sam had totally stopped inhaling the dessert and his mouth hung open in amazement. Clearing his throat, he said, "Go on."

Max took a sip of water and continued.

"I left State Accounting to pursue a partnership and created Bingo City Flea Market. Our 50,000-square-foot building housed a four hundred seat bingo hall, three restaurants, and two hundred vendor spaces. What we needed most, an outdoor selling area, was not available, and so eventually we closed the venture. To some, this experience might seem disastrous. Yet for me, it was life changing. The closing of Bingo City Flea Market forced me to quickly find a new job, that turned out to be one of the first steps toward establishing my own wealth management financial consulting business. Rather than accept an offer to work at Smith Barney, I chose instead to work with my brother at PaineWebber. Here was an opportunity to work with someone who knew me and believed in me! So, while I worked and pursued the education and licenses necessary to become a financial planner, Katie helped support our family by becoming a successful realtor. Yet my employment at PaineWebber became tenuous because I was away from my desk and out of the office so frequently. Where was I? Rather than waiting for the telephone to ring, I was out meeting clients and building relationships. Though I never labeled it *'Peopletizing'* at that time, that's exactly what I was doing! My experiences at PaineWebber reinforced the lessons from high school tennis: focus and strategy, and also led me to the realization that I wanted to establish my own financial planning and consulting firm. Although some questioned my abilities, I took the plunge. The Max Wealth Financial Group started small—and today it is an extraordinarily successful business. We work as a team, advising clients and managing more than $100 million in assets, and grossing more than $1,000,000 annually."

Sam's jaw dropped even further. "$100 million dollars?"

Max winked. "Yes...but don't forget, I said '*more than*' $100 million.' Sam, my life story is not meant to generate sympathy or envy. It's just my story, and every life experience has brought me to the place I am at today. Just like your life has brought you to lunch today. From a place of few connections, I've developed innumerable relationships and associations by listening and by helping. From a place of struggle and deficit, I've worked hard to learn, experiment, and not be diminished by failures. In my life, struggle created passion. Success has brought me pleasure, yet I do not rest on my laurels. I continuously remind myself of the importance of every day, and with an eye to the future, I still seek new challenges and opportunities. What I know most of all is this: what I am, what I know, and what I do emanated from everything that happened in my life—and this is the philosophy that continues to guide my life. While I am proud of my accomplishments, I am still humbled by the place I find myself. I only hope that the time, the affection, and the support that I give others can in some small measure reflect the time, affection, and support that was—*and continues to be*—provided to me. Because it is in giving that I continue to learn to accept the affection and support of my family, friends, clients, and professional acquaintances.

"Helping others succeed is my mantra, Sam. It is the key to my own success. So, even though I have had some rough spots-Katie and I divorced a few years ago-I learned that people come in and out of our lives for reasons and seasons, and I have heard "no" more often than "yes." I continue on with the true knowledge that I can make a positive difference in the world. My work with wealthy clients and charities led me to investigate the calling of auctioneering, and it turns out that not only do I know numbers, I know how to move people to donate money for great causes. It's become my great passion. From a little kid with ADD in special education classes, to fighting on the playground, to a difficult upbringing, to the rough road of college and the difficulty of starting my own business in a very challenging field, I'm able to sit here today with you and share my journey because of one really important truth, Sam."

Sam's eyes were wide opened, so were his ears. He felt like this whole experience had become some sort of cosmic set up. "Uh…what truth is that, Max?"

Max was satisfied that he had fully delivered the main message, sat back in his chair, put both of his hands on the table, looked directly into Sam's eyes and said…

"If I can do this, imagine what you can accomplish."

*"We make a living by what we get,
and a life by what we give."*

-9-

The Reminder

Sam looked at his watch; he couldn't believe how quickly 90 minutes had flown by. The conversation with Max had been downloaded into his mental hard drive, and for some reason, he felt twenty pounds lighter than when he entered The Red Ram, even though he must have put on some weight judging by the size of the banana split.

"Time to go, Sam?" Max asked.

"Yes, I mean no, I mean, that I'm not sure. All of this is far more than I expected when I agreed to meet you for lunch. That auction seems like a year ago even though it has just been a few hours. It's like time has sped up and stood still all at once, if that is even possible," Sam stammered.

"It's possible," Max laughed. "That's always been an indicator to me that something bigger than my ego is at work."

"I don't experience that much at the supermarket," Sam countered.

"I've said that so much of how you experience life is a matter of perspective, Sam. That job is merely a reflection to some greater or lesser degree of how you see yourself, your abilities and value. That's not to say that there isn't a time and place for working in the produce department; it means that you really don't get in life what you deserve, *you get what you are*. Not good or bad, just a matter of consciousness. As I said before, if you work 60 hours a week stacking tomatoes and it brings you great joy, then it's where you should be. If not, then perhaps *a change is in order*."

Sam nodded that he understood.

"I've given you some important ideas about how to change your life. May I pass along the biggest roadblock to success?"

"Absolutely."

"I mentioned the 'ego' a few minutes ago. A major detriment to moving forward is in direct proportion to how inflated your ego becomes based on the results you produce, especially when it comes to money. A few weeks ago, I was at a business after-hours event, a meet and greet for wealth managers. At one point I was in a group of five people, and as we were discussing business, this guy walks up and starts spouting off about how much he has sold in terms of products, how he was able to cut corners and bend the rules for his own personal gain and profit. The guy went on for five minutes about his success, and how he had sold the business to his son and cashed in big time. He totally dominated the conversation as the rest of us just stood there listening to him describe himself in the most exaggerated manner, and it occurred to me that his ego, or '*the false self,*' had totally taken over. When he left our group, he found another in a different part of the room, and he started all over again. While it would be easy to dismiss him as a blowhard, he was really a reminder in disguise, a teacher of sorts with very important lessons."

Sam waited. "A teacher?"

"Never compare yourself to anyone else. Never assume that because someone has made vast amounts of money that they did it with integrity and, most importantly, understand that *you can't outrun your own created karma.* After I left that meeting, I stopped by my office, and out of curiosity I did a *Google* search on the guy and found out that he had been disbarred from his role as a wealth manager, was being investigated by numerous agencies for similar activity and may end up on the hook for $7 million dollars or even prison time." Max said, leaning forward towards Sam for even greater effect.

"Remember Bernie Madoff?"

"Yes, I did see that name in the news," Sam responded.

"Madoff started his firm with $5,000 he saved from working as a lifeguard. He would go on to control billions of dollars in assets and serve as the NASDAQ's chairman in 1990, 1991, and 1993. At some point in his life, his ego took over and it cost him big time. He is now serving 150 years in prison, one son committed suicide after being implicated along with other members of his family who were part of the coverup. Thousands of people were wiped out financially, and a few took their own lives because of him. The allure of the ego is strong; the lies of the ego are even stronger."

Sam was sitting with his eyes a bit glossed over, this was something to pay attention to, even more so than the "good" life lessons.

"There should only be one person you strive to be better than, Sam. Your goal should be to become a greater person than you were yesterday, but not as great as you can be tomorrow. Your ego will attempt to lure you away from all of that, but you should follow your heart in all things, and judge your success not by what you have, but rather by your own ability to overcome adversity and impact yourself and others in a positive way. Success, as you define it, will follow."

"I don't even know what to say at this point, Max. I came to lunch wondering why in the world you would give a guy like me the time of day, only to find out that we are more alike than different. All through this short time together I've not just learned about you, but I think I have learned a great deal about myself: how much I have let circumstances define me instead of reveal me, and that I'm my own worst enemy. I stopped taking chances and settled because it felt safer to do so, but I made my life so much smaller than it could have been. Fear of change, fear of what might happen, and *fear…of…success* on any level might be what holds me back more than anything else. I don't even know where to begin to thank you. I have some serious thinking to do about my life, what is possible for me, and how to move forward."

Max took a sip of water just as the waiter came with the bill. "Sam, how much do you think this lunch was worth? I'm not talking about what is on the bill, but for you personally?"

Sam squirmed a bit as he always did when it came to a question like this. Then all of a sudden, the image of Jill raising her hand and committing to thousands of dollars for a blank piece of paper came to mind.

"I would say that the value of this lunch and all that you have shared with me is exactly what I think it is, not more, not less, and that how I put to use what you have given me will be to a great extent, a determining factor of the value of our conversation."

Max beamed.

"Right answer…and because you got it right you can pay for lunch!"

Sam gulped, took out his debit card and opened up the small leather binder and looked at the bill.

"PAID" was neatly stamped in red ink over the amount of $144.50.

"I have an account here Sam. The bill was paid before we even sat down. But the most important thing is that you were willing to pay for what you were served, and that is already progress in my opinion," Max assured him. "Well done; *however, you can leave the tip.*"

Sam reached back into his billfold, took out a twenty-dollar bill and without hesitation put the money in with the check and looked at Max directly.

"*Thank you*," Sam said, and for the first time in years, he meant it.

"The difference between living an up and down vertical life and shifting to a much broader horizontal life is about awareness and gratitude. Expanding the boundaries of belief creates space for abundance in many forms."

-10-

Meeting of the Minds

As the men stepped out into the bright sunlit afternoon, Max asked Sam if he might just have a little more time before he went home. Seeing how the day had gone so far, Sam agreed, noting that he had taken the day off. With that, Max lifted his hand and the black sedan, with Seth behind the wheel, pulled up to the curb and they both got in.

"Do you mind if I ask where we are going?" Sam inquired.

"The Mastermind Group is meeting today. We are a little late but if nothing else, you can get a taste of what it's like to be around people who think very differently than you do, and because of that, their lives are full, abundant and thriving."

"Thriving?"

"Yes, that's the *opposite* of surviving, Sam. Most people just survive when they could thrive instead," Max declared.

Twenty minutes later they pulled up to a long brick building that housed many different companies. Seth dropped them off right at the front door. Max led the way to a large conference room and looked through the glass doors. Inside sat four people, two men and two women, with notepads. Max knocked and entered with Sam in tow.

"Ladies and gentlemen, I apologize for being late; this is my new friend, Sam Paige." Max announced.

A short- haired woman stood up, her eyes bright blue behind her glasses, and extended her hand to Sam. "I'm Bettie Archer. Very nice to meet you," Sam was struck by the strength of her grip.

Then came a tall, thin fellow who was wearing a tailored suit. "Greetings, I'm Richard Cohen."

Right behind Cohen was a blond woman with squared shoulders and bracelets that made her arm jangle when she reached to shake hands. "Nessa Rogers. Pleased to meet you, Sam."

The last to stand was a man who looked vaguely familiar but Sam couldn't quite place him. Athletically built, in his fifties, buzzcut and thick across the chest. "Well, Sam, nice to meet you. I'm Terry Hoffman."

The name rang a bell.

"Terry Hoffman?" Sam said out loud. "From *Chicago Sports Magazine*?"

"One and the same," Hoffman responded. "I take it you are a reader?"

"Well, where I work, we have a magazine aisle, and now and then I read your articles when on my break," Sam said, suddenly reminded of twelve-hour days stacking produce. "I enjoy it, yes."

"Enough shop talk boys," said Nessa. "We were just discussing the PFFC process when it comes to setting and reaching goals."

They all found their seats at the broad table and on the large white board on the wall were four words written in bold marker:

Patience, Faith, Focus, Clarity.

Max spoke up.

"Those four words, so very powerful. It's a reminder to me that *if you do in life what is easy, life is hard. If you do in life what's hard, life is easy.* In order to create something from nothing, you must have a cornerstone from which to create. We live in a time when people have very little patience for the process of life. We want instant gratification without having to pay the price. Patience is often the price one pays for reaching a worthwhile goal."

Bettie, Richard, Nessa, and Terry nodded in approval. Sam simply sat as he did for most of lunch, just listening.

Nessa added, "Faith has been defined in many ways but for me it's always been a verb, an action word. It means taking steps that are necessary, even though I might not understand the process or have all my ducks in a row. I learned a long time ago that *the ducks are never all in a row*, and if you wait for them to line up, you will never have the faith to move forward."

Terry spoke up and confirmed Nessa's words. "As a writer, I have a deadline to meet for every issue of the magazine, a clearly defined goal. But even though I might have a lot of information at my fingertips, the actual writing is exactly this process. I have faith that the right words will come as needed; and patience to allow for that process to take place. Readers have no idea how much I rely on patience and focus to allow a blank computer screen to fill with words. My patience gene has been tested many times, but it's like a muscle. The more I work it out, the stronger it gets over time."

Max was about to chime in but Richard spoke first.

"All of these words are important. Any one of them can instantly change your mindset which isn't always easy to do with the bombardment of negativity in the world. Every time I come to our Mastermind Group and see those four words, I am once again centered in myself. For me, clarity is essential. For years I was all over the map in regard to my purpose in life. I was stuck in a job I hated, and even though the money was good, I ate well, but didn't sleep well and it took its toll. When I ran into Max Farber, all that changed. When he gave me that little book he wrote, that started to help me get focused on what I wanted out of life, rather than what people wanted out of me. I realized pretty quickly that everyone is dispensable in the corporate world."

Sam cleared his throat and took a sip of water from the glass in front of him. "May I ask you a question, Richard?"

"Sure."

"This all sounds great but, what is a *Mastermind Group* anyway?"

Max looked around the table, and before he could answer, Bettie smiled at Sam and said, "Apologies to you. We've been doing this for so long that we just take it for granted we all know what we are here for. Sam, have you ever heard of Napoleon Hill?"

Sam shook his head no.

"Well," Bettie continued, "He was a man who had experienced great failure in his life until one day in 1925, he figured out some basic principles in an eight- volume book series called, *The Law of Success*. He introduced the concept of two or more people joining together to solve problems," Bettie said.

Max added, "In 1937, Hill wrote one of the greatest books on personal achievement, *Think and Grow Rich* and he expanded on the theory that a group of people, working in harmony is a 'mastermind,' and by supporting each other we all move forward towards success. We hold each other accountable and encourage each other to set goals, reach for higher ground, and make the world a better place. A side effect, of course, is wealth, but as you have been finding out, abundance is measured in many ways."

"I've never heard of anything like this. Nobody I work with talks about this stuff. Richard, one more question. How did you know what you wanted out of life?" Sam asked.

"Well, Sam, the first step was to figure out what I didn't want in my life. The people, places and negative situations that had me stuck in place. I actually made a list one day of all the things that I felt needed to be eliminated for me to have some chance of living a greater life experience. It wasn't easy to make the needed changes, but far better than how I had been living, so far below my potential. Then, with those four words as my guide, I began to focus on what I wanted, worked to maintain clarity and focus and develop the patience needed for the process to take place. As Max said, patience is essential to allow the universal tumblers to be put in motion that which you are seeking."

Then Terry jumped in. "Sam, asking better questions is one of the most important parts of the PFFC equation. For example, here's a list of questions I am constantly asking myself. What is the best way today to build trust? What does leadership mean to me? How will I handle the negative people in my life today? Am I willing to follow my 'gut instinct' and not just my mind? Am I being impeccable with my word, to myself and others? Am I willing to ask for help and guidance when needed? And perhaps, most importantly, what limiting beliefs are holding me back?

Max looked at Sam and said, "Sound familiar?"

Sam nodded his head, yes.

Max continued. "No one in this room was dropped off on the planet as we are today. All of us have done the work needed to overcome adversity, break stereotypes, heal our inner wounds, and turn our scars into stars. The limiting beliefs are blessings in disguise, an opportunity for growth and change. So, while we meet twice a month to share our successes, we are also very aware that each of us are still a work in progress. That's how life is. But it's all a choice. Free will. Just remember you can either be a victim of change or a participant, but not both at the same time. Each one of those choices will give you a result, one is more powerful than the other."

Sam felt a surge of energy as Max was speaking. He sat up a bit straighter in the chair, and the words that came from his mouth seemed to be from some other place, a long-forgotten file drawer marked, "Hope."

"Do you think it's possible that I might be able to attend these Mastermind Group meetings when my schedule permits?"

Nessa challenged him. "Sam, we would be glad to have you join us. Might I suggest that you make this group a priority? It's too easy to let outside circumstances determine our participation. All of us are now on very tight schedules, but we understand that without these conversations, we could easily get sucked back into the chaos of life and forget how important it is to be connected to a support system that allows all the rest in our lives to be so abundant. Think of it as an investment in yourself and your future. The dividends are worth the time spent."

Bettie went up to the white board and grabbed the marker. "Sam, which of these four words do you connect with most today?"

Sam didn't even have to think about it.

"Faith. I've lost faith in myself, in my abilities, and as a result, most of the time I feel hopeless, that my life won't be any better than it is today, or at least how it's been up until the moment I met Max."

They all smiled.

Bettie put a big circle around the word and then walked over to Sam and gave him a red marker. "Write it in the palm of your hand, Sam. It's a great little reminder that has helped me many times over the years."

Sam took the pen, wrote *FAITH* in his right palm and then Max exclaimed, "Bravo, Sam!"

The others in the room clapped loudly. Sam felt like, somehow, he turned a corner that he didn't even know was there.

As the clock on the wall nudged towards three, the meeting was about to adjourn until Max figured he would drive home one more point for the day.

"Before we all head back to our lives, just one question. How many of us made our bed this morning?"

With smiles on their faces, Bettie, Nessa, Richard, and Terry all raised their hands. Max looked at Sam and then raised his hand as well.

Before they all left the room, Bettie came up to Sam and out of her bag produced a copy of, *Think and Grow Rich* and opened up the front cover. There on the facing page was scrawled, *Napoleon Hill*, and the author had pushed hard into the paper with a pen, his autograph making a permanent indentation.

"Wow," Sam remarked. "That's really something."

"Yes, it is" Bettie said, extending the book out to Sam who was dumbfounded. "When you are ready, pass it on to someone else."

Max smiled, put his hand on Sam's shoulder and said, "C'mon, I'll give you a ride home."

-11-

The Shift

Sam could hardly fall asleep after the day he had with Max, even though he was mentally and emotionally exhausted. He tossed and turned all night, glancing now and then at the baseball in the cube on the nightstand that gleamed like a small lighthouse beacon in the pitch-dark room. Max's words and ideas were stuck in him like splinters of truth, and on some level, they actually hurt, because deep down, Sam knew that he had gone off course many years ago.

He had let the circumstances of his life determine his path, which is exactly the opposite of what Max was offering in the form of his "Abundant Life Roadmap." The ideas sounded good in theory, but Sam kept wondering how in the world to put the concepts into practice, especially since he had to get up in a few hours and begin the task of stocking produce as he had for so many years.

He also realized that Jill had not called after the meeting with Max. He found himself hoping that she would be working the deli so he could see her when he arrived at the supermarket.

Sam finally nodded off when the bell on his phone rang, indicating a text message had come in. He ignored it and rolled over, but after a time he gave up and grabbed the phone. Turning it on, the screen brought a glow to the room, and there in the message file subject line, he read, "*Apprentice Opportunity - Max.*"

"What the…" Sam grumbled under his breath. He sat up, turned on the light, and he noticed the time on his phone was 3:42 a.m. "Geez, doesn't this guy sleep?"

Sam rubbed his eyes, opened the text message, focused as best he could, and read the message aloud.

"*Good Morning, Sam! I was honored to spend some time with you yesterday and after I dropped you off at home the thought came to me that since I have an auction this Friday, perhaps you would consider the position of my "apprentice" and help me make the event a success!" You have what it takes! Just let me know asap. Regards, Max.*"

Sam sat quietly on the edge of his bed and read the message again, slowly as if to let the words sink in deeper. Images of some sort of indentured servitude came to mind with the word "*apprentice*" and he couldn't even begin to imagine a scenario where he would be working within arm's reach of Max Farber. Lunch was *life changing* but something like this, could be, *life altering.*

He also knew that sleep would have to wait. Perhaps he'd catch a nap while waiting for the delivery truck to arrive in that spot above the walk-in freezer by the loading dock later in the morning. As he lay back down on the bed contemplating the text, he remembered that little book Max had given him. He got up, fished the book out of the inner pocket of his coat, and in the kitchen made a pot of coffee.

"Might as well read a bit," Sam said to no one in particular.

As the coffee pot began to bubble and hiss, Sam plopped down in a chair, turned on the light and randomly opened to a page with the quote:

"Optimism is the faith that leads to achievement." Helen Keller

Sam turned the page and continued reading.

"Whether the endeavor is personal or professional, the *Peopletizer* works from a foundation of philosophy, goals and plans. 1) *Articulate a life philosophy.* To build and sustain a life of quality, it is important to articulate a personal and professional philosophy."

"I don't have either one," he said to himself. "Maybe I should start." With that he got up, found a legal note pad used for scribbling and tore off the top sheet. He grabbed a pencil, with a small rush of excitement.

Continuing to read:

2) *Create written goals and a daily 'to do' list.* It's easier to reach a goal-*any goal*-if you have committed to it in writing.

3) *Always have a five-year plan.* Five is the magic number" wrote Farber. "Remain focused but flexible, patient but persistent, and above all, look for the little growth indicators that you are on the path of your choosing."

Sam wrote at the top of the legal pad, "*My Life Philosophy,*" and then thought for a moment or two and began to write:

"My life philosophy is that no matter what happens to me, I am in control of my response. Furthermore, no matter how many times I have failed in the past, today is another day, a chance to begin again. I will invest my time and efforts into those things that serve me well, and I will then be served in return. In addition, I will always give 100% to any effort, I will surround myself with talented people from whom I can

learn, and I will encourage others to grow and learn as well."

Stunned by what had appeared on the page, almost as if written by some unseen hand and surely from a higher place within, Sam was awash with emotions. All at once, he was scared as never before; but at the same time, a sense of elation swept over him as if he was a young boy, waiting in line for the rollercoaster ride.

He flipped over the paper and on the next page wrote: "Goals."

"In five years, I will be working at a job that values my time and talents and I am compensated accordingly. I will be taking night and weekend classes to earn a college degree. I will be living in a nice home with a big backyard and a pool, and a garage. I will be driving the car of my choice, getting a paid vacation once a year, great benefits, wonderful co-workers and..."

Sam stopped in his tracks. What he wrote next was the biggest surprise of all.

"I would like to have Jill in my life."

As if a hot potato fell into his hand, Sam dropped the pencil and pushed it aside. "Where in the heck did that come from?" he wondered.

He glanced at the clock; an hour had passed very quickly. While it was still before his usual wake up time, Sam felt fully awake and realized that he had been sleeping through much of his life, even while he was upright and breathing. He grabbed the phone, and hit "Reply" on Max's text message.

"Count me in. Sam."

Then he pressed "Send" and got another cup of coffee.

As the sun began to rise, he read a bit more of the little handbook. As he went to shower, he reached to turn the radio on and then had a second thought. He turned off the morning news that brought nothing but all the bad things happening in the world, and instead, he simply enjoyed the warm water that cascaded down like torrents of rain. In short order, he was dressed and out the door, an hour early for work.

When he walked in the back door of the supermarket, Lonnie was there making out the next week's schedule. He looked up at Sam, glanced at his watch, then back again, unsure of what he was seeing.

Sam grabbed his time card and said, "What's up Lonnie? Hey, I need off early on Friday because I am going to be an auctioneer's apprentice, and so I am here an hour early this morning. Matter of fact you don't even have to pay me the $14 which is really just $10 after taxes. The first hour today is on me."

He spun on his heels and headed off to make sure that the bananas were stacked just so, and that the bin for navel oranges was full.

Not quite sure of what he just heard, Lonnie tapped his pencil on the desk, wrote "*Paige Early Out*" on the Friday space, sat back in his chair and said out loud, "Huh."

Jill arrived, punched the clock just a few minutes after Sam had left the office, and Lonnie barked, "Your man, Sam, might need a little therapy or something. He came in early, asked to get out early on Friday and said that he is working for nothing the first hour of the day. Something about only getting ten bucks after taxes and my guess is that…"

She put her hand up as if to stop Lonnie from speaking. "He doesn't need therapy, and you can guess all you want, but I know that Sam is heading in the right direction after our event earlier this week. Remember, it was you who made him reconsider accepting my invite."

Lonnie was a bit stunned.

"You talk too loud Lonnie, and in the deli I can hear just about everything that goes on in the bread aisle. I really appreciate you giving Sam a nudge in my direction."

While he tried to keep up his crusty exterior as a floor manager, Lonnie smiled and winked at Jill.

As she was opening up the cases to put out the cold cuts, suddenly Sam was standing at the counter.

"I thought I might have heard from you yesterday after lunch."

"I didn't want to interrupt your day, plus I had no idea how long you might be tied up. Did it go well?" Jill replied.

Sam thought about it and said, "I really can't put all of it into words. What I do know is that there is something in the works that doesn't have anything to do with stacking bananas. Maybe we can have lunch at the same time today, and I can share what happened."

"Are you asking me out to lunch?"

"I guess so," Sam smiled. "Know any place we can get a good deli sandwich?"

Even though he had been up most of the night, Sam wasn't at all tired. At lunch, he told Jill about all that had taken place at The Red Ram, how he learned Max was once like him, that Max gave him the little *Peopletizing Book* that he wrote, and the introduction to the Mastermind Group with some amazing people, and that the lady from the group gave him the, *Think and Grow Rich* book that was actually signed by the great Napoleon Hill!

Sam barely touched the sandwich Jill had made for him. He talked so fast about all that had transpired in just a few days and hardly took a breath while doing it. Finally, he stopped, snatched a big bite out of the corned beef on rye, shoved half a dill pickle down, and wiped his face.

Before Jill could respond to all of the breaking news, Sam jumped back in.

"Get this. Max asked me to be *his apprentice* this Friday evening at an event! I got a text message from him this morning, so early it was still dark! I told him I would do it! I'm getting off work early!"

Jill smiled and said, "Sam I am so very proud of you. Look how much has changed in just a few days."

Sam reached across the table, put his hand on hers and said, "Yes, it has."

-12-

The Apprentice

Friday couldn't come fast enough for Sam Paige. Never had he so looked forward to getting to work early, so he could leave work early and see what might lie ahead at the fundraising event as Max's "apprentice." The anticipation helped make the hours fly by, and while Jill had the day off, Lonnie was predictably standing at the time clock when Sam punched out, just to get in one more shot.

"Big night, Paige?" Lonnie cracked.

"Matter of fact it is," Sam responded. He felt that Lonnie was going to press further, but Sam was ahead of the curve. "Gotta go." With that, he slipped his time card in and out of the slot with a loud "clank" and rushed out the door.

By the time Max's driver, Seth, was texting him just forty-five minutes later, Sam was already showered, shaved and dressed in the clothes he bought for the event he attended with Jill just days before. Glancing in the mirror, he couldn't help but think about how much had changed in just a very, very short time.

The horn sounded at the curb, Sam bounded down the stairs and into the waiting black Lincoln, before Seth could get out and open the door for him.

"Hey Seth! Let's go…! Uh and by the way…where are we going? Where is this event?" Sam asked, while buckling up his seat belt.

"Well, Mr. Paige, have you ever heard of The Red Ram restaurant?

They both laughed.

"Yeah, I've heard of that place" Sam smiled.

In short order, and despite of the Friday afternoon rush hour, the car pulled up at the restaurant and in a déjà vu moment, Max Farber was waiting at the door to greet Sam once again.

"Well, there he is. Sam Paige, auctioneer apprentice extraordinaire," Max announced. "Good to see you my friend. C'mon in and let's go over the event check list."

"Sounds good," said Sam and with a backward glance to Seth who gave him a thumbs-up, off the two men went towards the banquet room. They opened the double doors revealing a room with seating for 450 people. Sam took a deep breath and followed Max up to the riser and podium.

"Sam, basically, you are my right arm tonight. Your job is to make sure I do my job which means keeping track of all the amounts raised on each item that guests will be bidding on in the live auction. Don't worry about the silent auction stuff, the volunteers will take care of that. It also means that you'll need to make sure that the water pitcher is full, as is my glass so I don't lose my voice. You will also be in charge of making sure that the winners get their prizes and in turn, collect their check, made out to the foundation, including any information that is required for follow up."

Sam looked a bit dazzled with all of that so Max added, "Tonight you are the gopher!" Seeing that his joke fell short, Farber said, "You know…*go for this*…and *go for that*!"

The ice broke, Sam Paige smiled, and suddenly the doors opened and the room began to fill with patrons supporting The Special Kids Network, a fundraising arm for several charitable organizations that assist children with special needs. The buzz in the room was palpable, much like it was when he and Jill attended the event he had first met Max at days earlier.

Sam had gone from guest to participant, from observer to student, and from the produce department to a seat on the main stage. A feeling of deep gratitude began to overtake Sam. He forgot what it felt like to be part of something bigger than himself. Max happened to catch Sam taking it all in, and he knew that the wheels of change had been put in motion once again.

Just as he had many times before, Max summoned up his talent for connecting with large crowds of people, making each of them feel as if he was talking to them personally, a skill that Sam marveled at. As the dutiful apprentice, he made sure that Max had what he needed as he pounded the gavel time and time again, his energy reaching a new crescendo for each auctioned item, exhorting those holding paddles to outbid each other as made the case for kids with special needs, and how every single dollar raised would change their lives for the better.

It was a whirlwind evening.

Sam was diligent in his efforts to make sure he kept track of the winners and the amounts, thankful that all of his years of counting oranges and peaches were paying off in a big way. As the night continued, he was caught up in the energy of the event, with Max pulling 500 people, including patrons and volunteers along for the ride of their lives.

In just over an hour, a record amount of *one million dollars* was raised, that would be split evenly over programs that made a concrete, constructive difference for kids who were the recipients. Sam followed up with the last few bidders who gladly made out checks in amounts that boggled his mind.

As the room emptied, he turned to see a steady stream of well-wishers thanking Max for his efforts, for being the catalyst for such a positive change in the world.

That is when the big "AHA" hit him right between the eyes like a bolt from the blue.

Sam Paige could not go back to his old life again.

All that had transpired since Jill asked him to attend the fundraiser, *all of it* was in some way shape or form an opportunity in disguise from the universe to become a new man. He had been shown through Max what is possible if he chose to go past his self-imposed limitations. He had learned from Jill how to transform pain into gain by making good on a promise. The taxi driver who quoted Emerson, finding the right clothes at Goodwill, the Ernie Banks baseball, and even Lonnie had played a magical role by goading Sam into accepting Jill's invite. All the puzzle pieces had been put into place, and all he had to do was make the decision to say, "*Yes*," which would lead him to the next piece of the roadmap. There he stood, not three feet way from Max, who used to be him at one time many years ago.

Incredible.

Finally, the stage cleared, Max stuck out his hand and said, "Sam, outstanding support! We raised a record amount of money tonight as a team and I couldn't have done it without you!" With that, Max opened an envelope and pulled out a check.

It was made out to Maxwell Farber in the amount of $10,000.00, the same amount that Jill had donated just a few nights earlier. "It's my fee for auctioneering this event, Sam. To be clear, I wasn't paid for raising money, I was paid for helping people. It's my mission in life and with that comes abundance in many forms."

Sam understood and nodded his head in agreement.

Then Max reached into the pocket of his jacket, pulled out another envelope that had Sam's name on it and said, "This is for you."

Sam opened it up and pulled out a thick wad of $100 bills that totaled $1,000.00 and a note inside that read, "*Sam, thank you for being my apprentice this evening. I've learned a great deal from you. Remember, what you focus on the longest, becomes the strongest."*

Speechless, Sam looked at Max and before he could say "thank you" the auctioneer said, *"You're welcome."*

EPILOGUE

The day after the event, Sam summoned up a serious amount of courage and gave his two weeks' notice. When he punched out on his last day of work, Lonnie stood at the time clock smirked, "You'll be back Paige, mark my words."

Sam just smiled and said, "Yes, I will. But not as an employee. I have a new opportunity Lonnie."

Only Jill knew that Sam had accepted a full-time position in Max Farber's office as his official *"apprentice"* that allowed him to earn more money than he would stacking veggies, but also this opportunity came with a price tag. Sam had to agree to immerse himself in *"the betterment of humanity"* and commit to the Mastermind Group, an invite he didn't hesitate to accept. He began to learn that there is no such thing as "free time" because time is the one commodity for which we cannot put a price tag, Sam dove into online courses that would eventually lead him to a degree in business development, something born out of all the conversations in his head at the supermarket when he felt he could improve customer service, but wasn't in a position to do so.

Six months later Sam had a fair amount of money in the bank. Max had helped him put together his *Abundant Life Roadmap* and now that his financials were a bit more in order and his professional life was beginning take shape there was one more piece of the puzzle to put in place personally.

Walking into the supermarket Sam carried the energy of a man ten years younger, much to the notice of his former co-workers. Lonnie caught sight of him and came over in a few quick steps, and by chance, caught up to him in the produce department, where Sam had spent so many years.

"I was right about you, Paige. I said you would be back," he barked.

"Nice to see you too, Lonnie. Is Jill working today?"

Lonnie blinked twice and said, "Uh yea, she is."

"Thanks. Take care."

Sam spun on his heels, leaving Lonnie standing next to a bin of radishes.

"Never liked those things," Sam thought to himself.

Rounding the corner past the packaged meats, he saw Jill waiting on a customer, her blond hair swept back and up, her features sharp and bright.

He took a number, and when Jill was finished with the customer, she said out loud, "*Number 14?*"

Sam Paige grinned and said, "That's me."

Jill brushed back a strand of hair from her forehead, and with a big smile on her face, put her hands on her hips and said, "Well, Mr. Paige. How can I help you?"

Sam put the crumpled ticket in the small wicker basket on the counter, thought for a moment and then said,

"*What are you doing for the rest of your life?*"

"If you want something, create it."
Chad Coe

ABOUT THE AUTHOR

Chad Coe was mistakenly thrown into the world of special education at an early age. Chad, unlike many, overcame all he experienced as a young boy and didn't allow his dysfunctional childhood to stop him from becoming a hardworking, kind and loving father, husband, and friend. He looks at life in a positive way as he knows it is one of the cornerstones to living an abundant life. He believes that a key to success is helping and giving to others. In the most difficult of times, Chad is grounded in a mindset that everything is going to be alright, no matter what life looks like in the moment.

He has turned every failure he has experienced into a learning lesson and shares his story with the thousands of people who have walked through his office door on a regular basis.

Chad is sought after nationwide as an auctioneer and has raised millions for charitable organizations such as Catholic Charities, The Cystic Fibrosis Foundation, The YMCA, National Alliance of Mental Illness (NAMI) and many others. Chad believes his job is to *"inspire audiences to give"* and he works tirelessly with each client to plan entertaining benefit auctions that are engaging while supportive of the organization's mission.

For more information: www.chadcoeauctioneer.com.

Using the principals outlined in this book, Coe Financial Group builds solid financial foundations for clients in the greater Chicago area with a focus on long term goals, individual attention and flexibility. As an experienced specialist in wealth management strategies, Chad specializes in structuring programs based on a client's personal values, goals, and risk tolerance. He works with his clients to bridge the gap between where they are and where they want to be in the future.

For more information www.coefinancial.com.

Chad is also a highly sought-after keynote speaker. He has keen insight into human interaction and how to make quality business connections is in great demand in today's "Relationship Economy." Through his Strategic Mastermind Groups, his goal is to use his enthusiasm, passion, optimism, and success strategies to inspire and empower others to joyfully live their greatest lives and achieve their career goals.

For speaking inquires and to obtain your personal Abundant Life Roadmap, please email: chad@chadcoespeaker.com.

This parable is based on the life of Chad Coe.

Fictional characters have been created to recount Chad's journey through the many life challenges and changes he has endured, and the countless obstacles he has overcome. Any resemblance to actual persons, living or dead, or actual events or locations is purely coincidental.